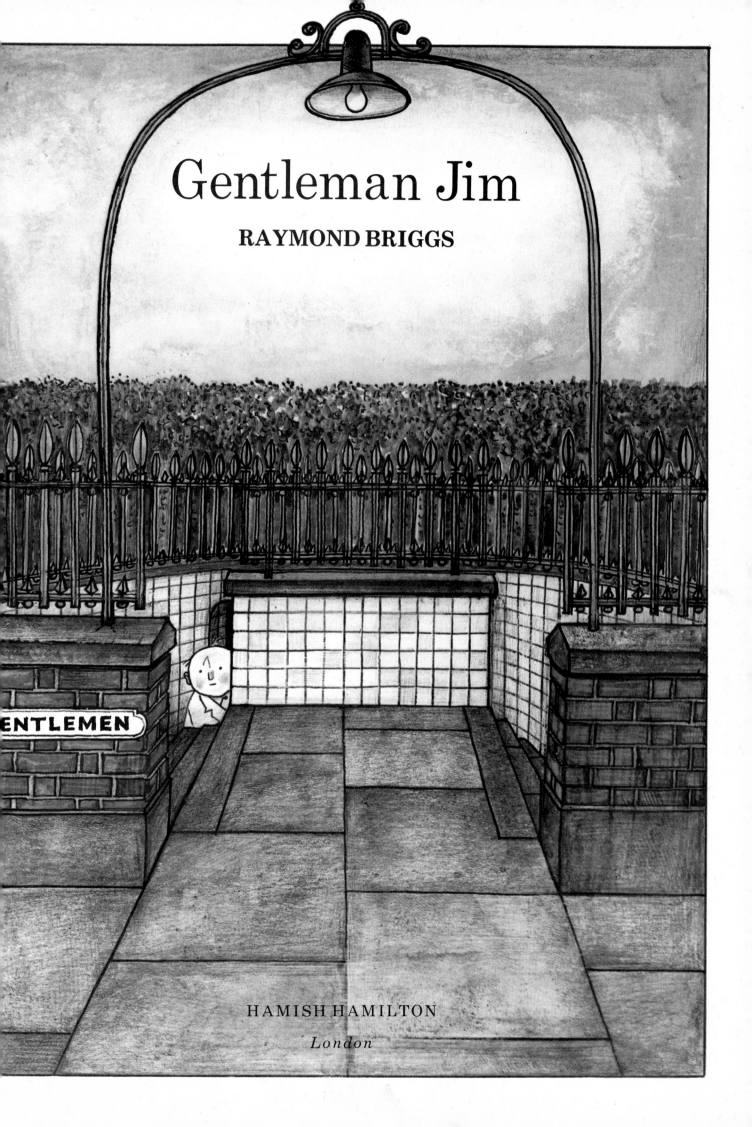

Gentleman Jim

RAYMOND BRIGGS

HAMISH HAMILTON

London

Other books by Raymond Briggs

THE STRANGE HOUSE
MIDNIGHT ADVENTURE
SLEDGES TO THE RESCUE
*

RING-A-RING O'ROSES
THE WHITE LAND
FEE FI FO FUM
*

THE MOTHER GOOSE TREASURY
THE FAIRY TALE TREASURY
*

THE ELEPHANT AND THE BAD BABY *text by Elfrida Vipont*
THE TALE OF THREE LANDLUBBERS *text by Ian Serraillier*
JIM AND THE BEANSTALK
*

FATHER CHRISTMAS
FATHER CHRISTMAS GOES ON HOLIDAY
FUNGUS THE BOGEYMAN
THE SNOWMAN

© 1980 Raymond Briggs
All rights reserved
First published in Great Britain 1980 by
Hamish Hamilton Childrens Books Ltd
Garden House, 57–59 Long Acre, London WC2E 9JZ

British Library Cataloguing in Publication Data
Briggs, Raymond
Gentleman Jim
I. Title
823'.9'1J   PZ7.B7646
ISBN 0 241 10281 2

Made and printed in Great Britain by
Redwood Burn Ltd, Trowbridge and Esher

Gentleman Jim

Time for a break...

...better look at the job opportunities...

Careers.... Let's see.. "Re-search-and Dev-el-op-ment Off-ic-er," mmm...

"Pro-duc-tion Dir-ect-or"

Every BOYS Story Book | Out in the SILVER WEST | The BOYS Book of PIRATES | CAREERS IN SURGERY | EXECUTIVE OPPORTUNITIES | The Monster Book for Boys | How to be a Diplomat

"Fi-nan-ci-al Con-troll-er..

"Eur-op-ean-In-ter-nal Aud-it-Man-ag-er. Crumbs!

"Man-power-Train-ing and-Dev-el-op-ment-Dir-ect-or-£18,000-plus-car" Crumbs! Triffic!

"ARE-YOU-A-DEC-IS-IVE-PER-SON?" No, s'pose not, really. Been thinking about changing this job for 12 years

"BE-AN-OFF-IC-ER-IN-THE-ROY-AL-MAR-INES Man-y-car-eers-will-use-the-tal-ents-you-have-The-Nav-y-will-use-those-you-don't-even-know-you-have."

Crumbs! I wonder what talents I have what I don't even know I have?

"battle-strat-eg-y-tech-niqu-es-of-guerr-ill-a-war-fare-wea-pon-tech-nol-og-y-mil-it-ar-y-spear-head-of-Roy-al-Nav-y-in-thick-of-act-ion-when-ev-er-Brit-ain-is-in-volv-ed def-end-ing-NA-TO's-North-ern-flank-seek-and-des-troy miss-ions-in-depths-of-jungle"- Crumbs!

Perhaps the Royal Marines Officers Course would unlock the key to my personality?

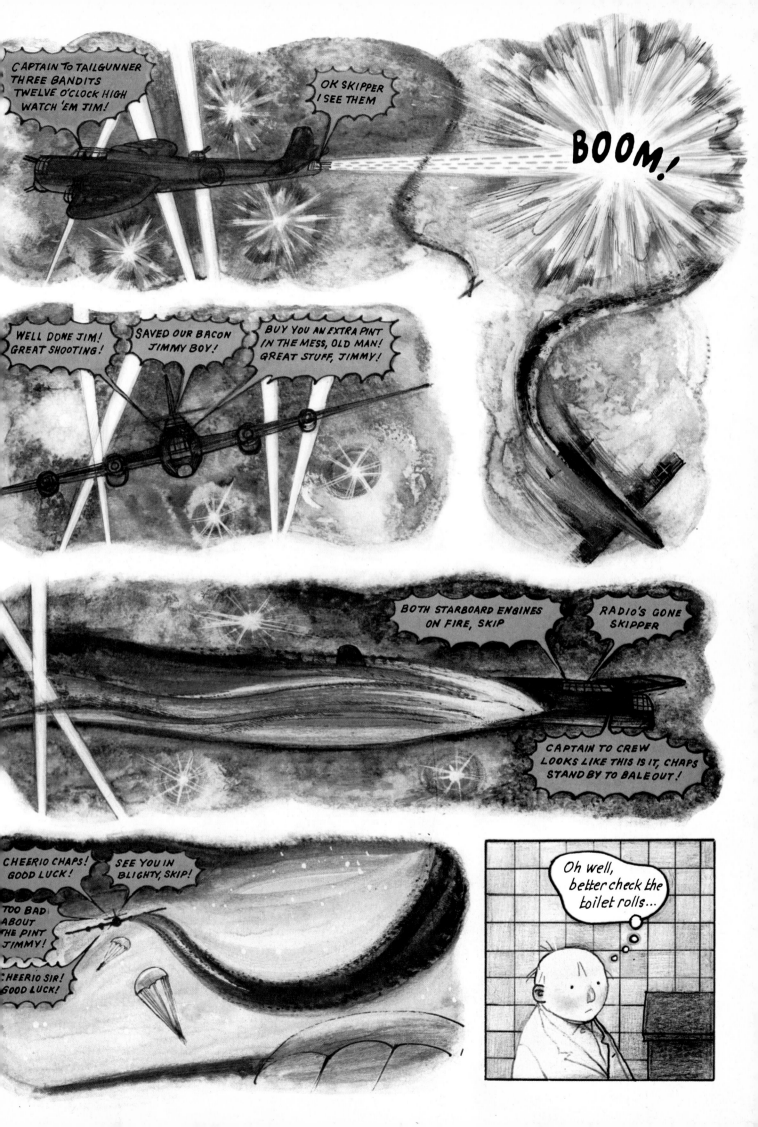

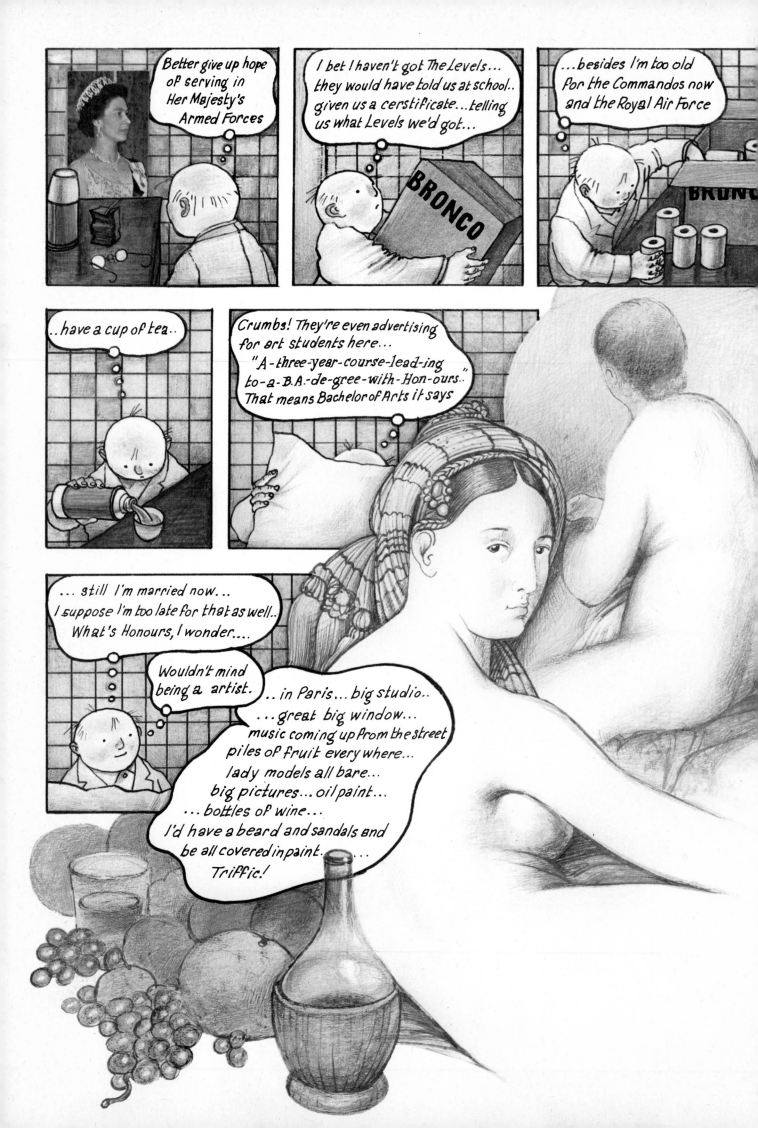

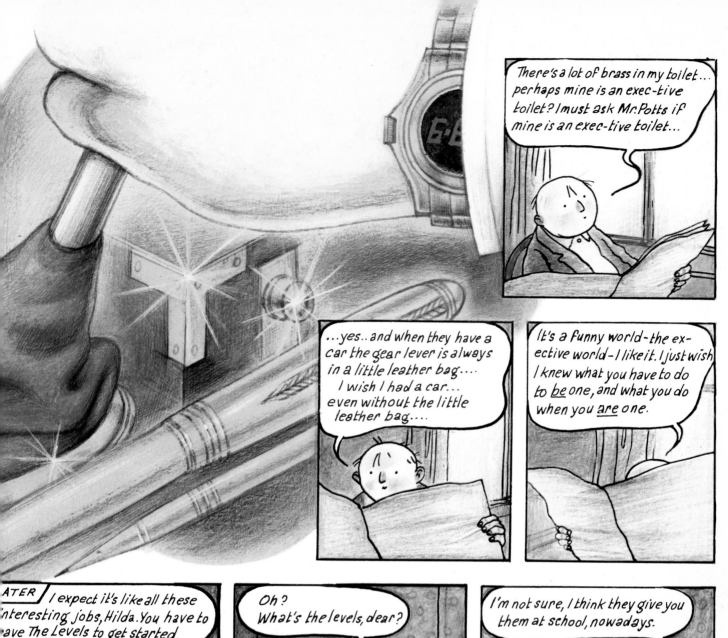

There's a lot of brass in my toilet... perhaps mine is an exec-tive toilet? I must ask Mr. Potts if mine is an exec-tive toilet...

...yes.. and when they have a car the gear lever is always in a little leather bag.... I wish I had a car... even without the little leather bag....

It's a funny world—the ex-ective world—I like it. I just wish I knew what you have to do to *be* one, and what you do when you *are* one.

LATER I expect it's like all these interesting jobs, Hilda. You have to have The Levels to get started.

Oh? What's the levels, dear?

I'm not sure, I think they give you them at school, nowadays.

I see, dear

They didn't give you any Levels did they, Hilda?

No, I don't think so, dear. They gave me a nice book, though.

Oh, what was it?

Prayers

Oh

NEXT DAY

Crumbs! Look! Real cowboy boots – spurs and all – only £5 Triffic!

£5 OFF
£62
£57

Gee! Thanks, pardner. These are swell.

Er, what is this, sir?

That's a five, buddy. The dough for the boots, OK?

But the boots are £57, sir.

£57!!! But it said £5 in the window!

£5 OFF, Sir. They were £62

Crumbs! I – er... I'll have to.. er... Withdraw from the purchase ...sorry....

Huh! Tripey shop! Boots will be cheaper out West... all those cows... cheaper leather ...I'll wait till the first pay day at the ranch... Get the six-shooter dinner time...

GET IN LANE

I wanna buy a Colt 45, bud. Goin' out West!

I'm afraid we haven't a Colt 45 at present, sir. There's a very nice Smith & Wesson 38 I could show you, sir.

Sure. A 38's OK with me, pal.

Here we are, sir, £96

£96! Crumbs! Haven't you got anything a bit cheaper, please?

By the way, sir, you do have a Firearms Certificate?

Er...no... going... ..out west..

U.S.A. sir?

No Texas

Then you will need an Export Licence as well as a Firearms Certificate, also Insurance, and, of course, a Customs Declaration, sir.

Oh, I see well.. I'd be better wait a bit then a firearms... expert... and a customs insurance... I see, sorry... I'd better make further enquiries....

Huh! Tripe! ..be easier to get a gun on The Range ...be lots of second hand... ..I'll wait till I get Out West.... see about the tickets after work

Ooh! There's a pistol! Real old one.

Oh - er, how much is the Highwayman's pistol in the window, please?

Highwayman?!! - Oh! The flintlock - a fine example, sir. Walnut with silver inlay, about 1720. It's £650, sir.

Crumbs! Have you got one a bit cheaper, please?

Yes sir, there's this sm... French one for only £32...

Oh - well, er... I meant.. ..about two or three pounds..

I should try a junk shop, sir.

Crumbs! Got to get a pistol. Can't be a highwayman without a pistol!

95 p
DEAD-EYE DICK
PISTOL
You too Can be a Marksman!

Dead-eye Dick.. ...Dick Turpin... perhaps that was the sort he had...

Yes, I'll have one, please. Any swords?

Yes sir. This nice little rubber one. Guaranteed not to harm the kiddies - 50 pence

Mmm... I can put kitchen foil round it so's it will gl... in the moonlight like cold steel...

FISHIN...

BAIT MAGGOTS NOW IN

Crumbs! Look! Highwaymen's boots!

How much are the Highwayman's boots in the window, please?

Eh? Oh! The boots - the waders you mean. £4 chum. Second hand. In good nick - only a few small holes. Try 'em on.

Pity they're not black.

You can always paint them - ha! ha!

Yes, that's an idea...

No spurs?

Spurs? On waders? You in a play or something?

No. I'm going to be a Highwayman.

Oh I see — fancy dress.

llo, dear

Hullo love, — look! I got a nice bit of black stuff for your cloak at the jumble sale this afternoon.

Oh, triffic!

Yes, and a nice bit of red for the lining. It'll be ever so romantic with a red lining.

Yes, and lacy cuffs they had, all aristocractic.

That old blouse of Mother's would do. I'll look it out.

he hat's difficult... there's Dad's old ARP helmet rom the war... could put bits of hardboard nd it to make it triangular.

The horse is a problem, dear. There's no horse shop near the Toilets.

It says on Telly to look in the Yellow Pages when you want something.

Yellow pages? What are they?

Well, it's like a telephone numbers book, only all yellow.

Oh, triffic! I'll do that tomorrow

an't wait to get started, Hilda! u see, you just have to hide hind the bushes and shout TAND AND DELIVER!" en you take all the gold!

Gold! Ooh, yes, lovely dear. Gold would be nice. I could have my hair done.

It wouldn't be for us, dear. It would be for The Poor.

ll, here she is, dear—
lack Bess!

My Goodness!
Is that the great black
charger?

Well, it's the best I could do
for the time being, my love.

We'd better put her in
the back garden.

I wish we had
a back entrance.

Are its feet clean?

Just a tick, dear.
I'll put some newspapers
down.

oh! My goodness!
ook what's happened!
od job I put the papers down

HEE! HAW! HEE! HAW!

The charger is making
a terrible noise, dear.
Perhaps it's hungry.
Have you fed it?

No, I never thought.
What does it eat?

Grass, I suppose.

Crumbs! Yes, it does!
It's finished the lawn.
I'd better take it up the Rec.

llo, 'ullo, 'ullo!
t 'ave we 'ere, eh?

Oh, it's my charger—Black Bess
Just giving her a feed.

A feed of Public Property, eh?

Well…just a bit of grass

Just a bit of Public Property
grass, eh? Muni-pical
Corporation Sports Field
grass, to be precise, eh?

Well,
I thought…

estruction of Muni-pical Corporation Sports
acil-ties, eh?
he Public Parks and Open Spaces Act of 1887
on't make no mention of Commonland
razing Rights, do it, eh?

Er….I'm sorry..I didn't get
The Levels…I don't know.

No. You don't know, but I do, Sonny Jim.
Your animal is also Fouling the Muni-pical Public Footpath,
and thus causing a Public Nuisance, innit eh?
You'd better come with me to The Offices, my lad.
I shall have to report this to the Muni-pical Authorities.

Crumbs!
Authorities!

I've left Black Bess outside for a bit...tied to a lamp post.

You do look pale, dearest. Whatever's the matter?

Oh dear, I'd better sit down. I feel quite done up...all shaky... I got properly told off up the Rec. An Official spoke very severely to me. He's reported me to the Muni-pical Authorities.

Never mind, love Have a nice sit down and a nice cup of tea, then you can tell me all about it.

LATER

Hullo! Knock at the door... I'll go...feel better now.

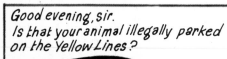

Good evening, sir. Is that your animal illegally parked on the Yellow Lines?

Oh yes! It's my new charger Black Bess. I'm going to be a Highwayman!

I see, sir. Well, the animal has been illegally parked for 27 minutes within the area of a Restricted Zone...

So I must serve this Official Summons upon you and request you to remove said animal from the vicinity.

YOU, THE ACCUSED DO HEREBY SWEAR

...but I live here...

I'm afraid that is entirely irrelevant, sir.

Is it because of The Levels?

Beg pardon, sir?

Is it because I haven't got any of The Levels?

I'm afraid I'm not with you, sir.

Could I leave her there if I'd got The Levels?

Sir! Not even an Offic— in Authority can Cause Obstruction o The Yellow Lines, sir

I might also caution you, sir, that said animal is Fouling The Pedestrian Footway. This constitutes an Offence which does not come within my Jurisprudence; however, it is my duty to inform The Police Department of the commital of said Offence.

Good evening, sir.

Crumbs! ....commital....

Who was that at the door, dear?

It was Someone in Authority. Another Official.

Oh my goodness!

They're after me before I've even started, Hilda. I expect it's due to modern security methods.

Oh dear!

What did he want, dear?

He's given me a Sums and he's going to commital me about the fence or something, he said.

I must keep Black Bess in the back garden, dear. Because the yellow lines are illegal.

Oh, I see, dear

NEXT DAY Good afternoon! Mr. Bloggs? Inspector Parker - jolly old R.S.P.C.A. We understand you are keeping a donkey here?

Yes, that's right. I'm going to be a Highwayman.

We've been informed that the jolly old donkey is insufficiently housed and inadequately fed. What?

No sir, not really sir...it's that at this moment in time I'm insufficiently organised at present, sir. I didn't know they eat all day, sir...

So the jolly old donkey is out in all jolly weathers? What?

Well, er...yes. Hilda won't have it in the house because of the — you know....

Well, Mr. Bloggs, I suggest you build a shelter for this jolly old donkey at once and see that it is fed and watered regularly....

...otherwise the jolly old R.S.P.C.A. will have to take jolly old legal proceedings against you. Is that jolly clear, what?

Yes, sir. Thank you, sir.

Good day!

Crumbs! Jolly old proceedings!

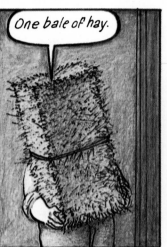

Mr. Bloggs? Good afternoon. Name — Morrison. Inspector — County Borough Council Local Urban District Offices — Surveyor's Dept. Understand structure erected back garden?

Er — oh yes. The stable. The charger is nice and warm now, thank you, sir.

Volume of structure in excess of 66·373 cubic feet? Yes?

Er, feet? What feet?

Regret. Must inspect. Measure. Yes.

Hmmm.... Yes. Structure approximately 279·90751 cubic feet. Illegal. Yes Furthermore no record heretofore of Planning Permission Application at County Borough Council Local Urban District Offices Planning Applications Dept.

...Er...I'm sorry, sir. I couldn't quite... ...follow...

Ha-ve-you-app-lied-for-Plann-ing-Per-miss-ion?

Er..what's plied for p'anning permission? Is it to do with The Levels?

Structure contravenes County Borough Council Local Urban District Bye-Law Building Regulations. Must be dis-erected forthwith.

Dis-...?

TAKEN DOWN, MAN!

But I've only just erect it up. The Royal Society for Cruelty made me.

Necessary dis-erect immediately or Council forced prosecute. Heavy fine plus enforced dis-erection.

Regret prosecute. Nice horse. Good afternoon.

Crumbs! ...prosticute!!

Who was that, dear?

Another Official in Authority. He says I've got to take the stable down.

Oh, my goodness!

Yes, it's because of its feet, or something. He's going to prosticute me if I don't.

Oh dear!

The Cruelty Man is going to do Legal Proceedings to me if it's not up, and the Planning Man is going to prosticute me if it's not down. Then there's the Muni-pical Authorities up the Rec. and the Sums from the Man in the Yellow Hat.

They've got The Law on me all round, Hilda. It's just like Gentleman Jim when the Bow Street Runners were after him.

The forces of Law and Order and Bow Street is closing all about me, Hilda. The net is tightening. I wish I had a rapier of cold steel!

I wonder if the Man in the Yellow Hat is a Bow Street Runner?

Never mind, dear. You haven't done anything wrong have you?

Oh, no. Nothing. I'm a free citizen and a Subject of Her Majesty. I'm innocent of all the preferred charges.

I'll be a quit in open court. They won't get me to yon gallows tree...

...but I'd better start robbing The Rich and giving to The Poor before they get me.

I'd better start this very night − er... i'faith!

Just going up to the bathroom to practice my silvery mocking laugh, for when I gallop away into the enshrouding darkness...

All right, my love. Don't be long − tea's nearly ready.

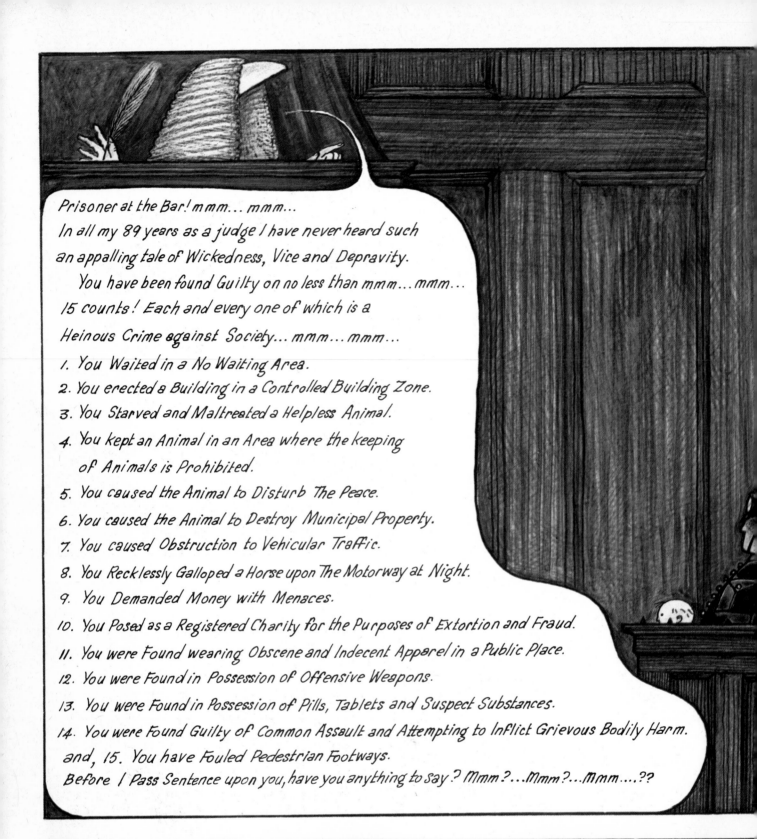

Prisoner at the Bar! mmm... mmm...
In all my 89 years as a judge I have never heard such an appalling tale of Wickedness, Vice and Depravity.
    You have been found Guilty on no less than mmm...mmm...
15 counts! Each and every one of which is a Heinous Crime against Society...mmm...mmm...

1. You Waited in a No Waiting Area.
2. You erected a Building in a Controlled Building Zone.
3. You Starved and Maltreated a Helpless Animal.
4. You kept an Animal in an Area where the keeping of Animals is Prohibited.
5. You caused the Animal to Disturb The Peace.
6. You caused the Animal to Destroy Municipal Property.
7. You caused Obstruction to Vehicular Traffic.
8. You Recklessly Galloped a Horse upon The Motorway at Night.
9. You Demanded Money with Menaces.
10. You Posed as a Registered Charity for the Purposes of Extortion and Fraud.
11. You were Found wearing Obscene and Indecent Apparel in a Public Place.
12. You were Found in Possession of Offensive Weapons.
13. You were Found in Possession of Pills, Tablets and Suspect Substances.
14. You were Found Guilty of Common Assault and Attempting to Inflict Grievous Bodily Harm.
and, 15. You have Fouled Pedestrian Footways.
Before I Pass Sentence upon you, have you anything to say? Mmm?...Mmm?...Mmm....??

...er...p..p..please, s...sir I..m..might have b..been..a..b.. better citizen If I'd had The L..L..Levels, sir...

What did you say?

WILL THE PRISONER PLEASE SPEAK UP!

..if I'd h..had L.. L..Levels, your Honours..

What is he saying for Heaven's Sake?

I'm afraid I've no idea, m'lud.

Dammit! It's nearly lunch time!

Then all that remains is for me...mmm to Pass Sentence upon you...mmm mm..bearing in mind your 37 years exemplary employment in-ah...er ...in...in your place of employment, I will be lenient with you...mmm...

mm..so..er...I...mmm er...mmm..mmmm.....

I... I... the........Sentence of the Court.... upon you is That you Be Taken from This Place to an Awful Prison-er-Lawful Prison and thence to a PLACE of EXECUTION and That you There be HANGED BY THE NECK UNTIL YE BE DEAD!!!

M'LUD!!! M'LUD!!!

.oh..er..no... I...I...I'll... start again...

Heh! Heh! Those were the days!

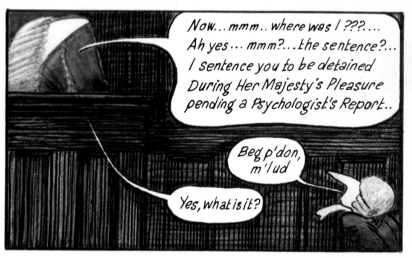

Now...mmm..where was I???....Ah yes...mmm?...the sentence?... I sentence you to be detained During Her Majesty's Pleasure pending a Psychologist's Report..

Beg p'don, m'lud

Yes, what is it?

t psychologist 'lud - sychiatrist

I said psychiatrist, dammit!

Yes, m'lud Of course m'lud Beg p'don m'lud

As I was saying...Her Majesty's Pleasure etcetera ....pending a psycho-thingummy's report ....take him away....

What's it like, dear?

Oh, it's not bad. It makes a change.

I've brought you a Robin Hood Annual and some Smarties.

Oh good, thanks. Triffic.

I might study for The Levels while I'm in here.

Oh, that's nice, dear.

Yes. I've found out I was right. They're only Education. There's Maths-that's like the sums we done at school, only modern. Then there's English - you know, spellin' an' that. And there's Modern Languages - sort of like the foreigners talk.

Oh nice, dear.

The Judge said it was for Her Majesty's Pleasure, didn't he?

Yes dear. Wasn't that nice?

Do they work you hard, love?

Oh no, it's cushy. They've put me on the toil! They say I'm an expert.

Oooh! It's nice to be an expert.

Yes, it'll keep me hand in.

It's taught me a lesson, Hilda. I realise now I got ideas above my station.

Station. Yes, dear. I mustn't miss my train.

I hope I can get my old job back when I come out.

BRRRRINNG! TIME'S UP.

I hope so, de...

Well, I'd better be off now. Goodbye, dear. God bless.

Goodbye, love.